WALKTHR

ON

TRIALS OF MANA

AKIN RICH

Copyright © 2019 Abraham Richards

All rights reserved. This book is copyright and no part of it may be reproduced, distributed, or transmitted in any form or by any means, including photocopying, recording, or other electronic or mechanical methods, without the prior written permission of the publisher, except in the case of brief quotations embodied in critical reviews and certain other noncommercial uses permitted by copyright law.

Printed in the United States of America Copyright 2019

Contents

Summary of the Game 1

Game Persona 4

    Intro to these characters 4

Beginning Lesson 10

Trials of Mana/Kevin's lessons 34

Trials of Mana/Angela's Lessons 43

Trials of Mana/Lise's Lessons 63

Trials of Mana/Carlie's Lessons 73

Trials of Mana/Part 1: The Legend of Mana 85

Trials of Mana/Part 2: The Mana Fairy 100

The Art of Killing Rabites 104

Trails of Mana/Part 4: Take the Golden Brick Road . 108

Trails of Mana/Part 5: A Gneed for Gnome 112

    Five Hacks in Choosing from Difficult Options 115

Trials of Mana
Summary of the Game

This copy for Trials of Mana features guides, plans or methods for the game, knowledge on the play persona, lessons on tasks, collection of information in the game, hacks, cheats, information and new developments regarding the play that Square Enix built and launched to be played on Microsoft Windows devices as well as Nintendo Switch and PlayStation 4.

The initial action representation name established in the year 1995 on the Super Famicom, has been modified to create Trials of Mana.

In this play, you will walk through the experiences of six special chief characters who have been joined together in order to defeat the evil dangerous creatures known as Benevodons (God Beasts). They are able to do this by getting the historical Sword of Mana.

You will experience live battles where the participant will be able to be in charge of three game personas of a team. The game personas move around the city or the rural areas to discover those places and come in contact with their rivals. They get to associate with those surroundings and items like secret routes and treasure boxes.

The special economic levelling that has been long expected, is a great feature that will be implemented in this series. The game personas are given the ability to move between the dark and light variants of types of tasks available to acquire more competencies and crafts.

❖ Upgrading

Any player that moves to a higher grade is given the option of persona traits that will be made better.

Strength: This trait tops up the injury inflicted by a casual strike done without sorcery powers.

Agility: This trait tops up the chances of opponents losing targets against you. Here, a lot of magic attacks need a level of skillfulness to be achieved else knowledge of them will not be acquired.

Vitality: This trait tops up protection and HP and reduces the injury gotten from a strike.

Intelligence: This trait tops up injury inflicted by sorcery powers, reduces injury gotten from opponent's sorcery attacks and boosts the chances of opponents losing their targets against you.

Spirit: This trait tops up the influence of sorcery attacks that are not aggressive.

Luck: This trait tops up the chances of crucial strikes and reduces the number of entrapments that can be inside spinning machines of jewel boxes.

Game Persona

There are six game personas that can be handled in Trials of Mana and the participant is to choose three to build a team. The opening of the game varies with each game persona. They also have various emotional qualities, unique competencies and materials. Even if you don't select some of the game personas, every of the six characters that came up initial will be featured in the play.

Intro to these characters

- ❖ **Duran**

Duran is a native of Forcena and a major sword fighter. I don't mean to pose him as a hero in some role-playing games but Duran's sword abilities can hardly be challenged by any person. Duran occasionally has a bad temper.

Duran is a courageous sword fighter and probably the game's most powerful persona. He is not particularly smart or clever. Duran's spell is the blade spell and he uses this to strike and cause component destruction with material strikes. He is great at ending battles with bosses quickly and his inability to dodges attacks faster can make him inconveniencing.

His lesson determines his eligibility for Shields to boost his ability to dodge better as well as cover him up. Strength is Duran's main status. Duran difficulty level is **Hard**

❖ **Hawk**

Hawk is a native of Navarre and a robber. He has a comic intelligence and hardly lets any valuable get past him. Hawk owns two sharp knives that help him strike an opponent two times.

Hawk is also called Hawkeye and he is a robber. It is expected that he is the game persona with the highest speed and wields two arms. With this, he is able to blow twice in one strike which lets him quickly release his techniques.

Hawk's lessons are quite sparse and they let him have access to special and helpful spells that make him really potential in the game. Agility is Hawk's Status.

- ❖ **Kevin**

Kevin is a mini human and mini beast. Kevin is a great warrior and his bodily strength is his only source of strength to destroy his opponents. He probably has a high HP with the possibility of learning how to restore health if he gets on the right lessons. He turns into a werewolf when it gets dark. The only status of his that can alter is his strength and it boosts at a very massive rate. Spirit comes out as the main status of Kevin.

Because of his beast and human nature, Kevin was cast out of the Beastmen. He and his dog now reside in the forest. The presence of Beastman blood in Kevin makes it possible for him to transform to a werewolf and boost his energy at nightfall. Kevin difficulty level is **Meduim**

❖ **Angela**

Angela is a pampered child of Altena's Queen. She does not have regard for orders and people in command but her sorcery abilities that will come up further in game are really exceptional.

Angela is the usual Black Mage but you can choose to call her Black Sorceress if it suits you better. She is the game persona with the exception to achieve her twelve sorcery skills available to her. These twelve sorceries can cause damage with six components. Except on rare cases, Angela rides on most bosses' low resistance to certain components to get a speedy end. Her bodily offense strikes are not really powerful but she has Intelligence as her main status.

❖ Lise

Lise is the warrior Princess and can be called Rise or even Rieze. Her position as the most general game persona is quite debatable although she has powerful material strikes and is skilful in spells to change status.

Summon spell is included in her lessons which helps her achieve a high destruction number. Although every group can have Lise as a member, newbie players might find it difficult to get the hang of Lise.

Lise is completely everything that Angela is not. Lise is born into a notable family and fights greatly with a spear.

She is probably the character with the best temperament. There is no specific status assigned to Lise.

❖ Carlie

Charlottle is a mini human and mini elf. She might not be the best warrior but she has health restoration power and is the one game persona credible enough to work as the White Mage. Charlottle is great at boosting the attributes of her associates. She speeds up the play session in any group she belongs to, with her health restoration powers. Spirit comes out as the main status of Charlotte.

Carlie occasionally acts less matured than the other game personas as she is the smallest in age among them. Heath was responsible for Carlie's upbringing because her parents died early. Carlie has turned the church in Holy City Wendell to her home. Her ability to restore health, is her major contribution to her team.

Beginning Lesson

> ➢ Warrior

Technology: The technology available here is the cross-slash ability.

Sorcery abilities: None

Although does not strike as fast as Hawk and Kevin, he possesses the strike with the highest effect in comparison with every other initial game persona. If his foremost lesson adjustment has not been completed, None will be unable to acquire sorcery abilities.

Foremost Lesson Adjustment

> ➢ **Light**: Horse Soldier

Technology: The technology available here is the cut-single target in three steps.

Sorcery Abilities: Present

- Knowledge

Heal Light: This allows only one aim.

The lessons on how to be a horse soldier are inclined towards protection than attacking. Duran is able to acquire defense armor and get knowledge on simple spells to restore health. The disadvantage is that Gladiator has more potent strikes than Duran in addition to the fact that he can only attack victim.

➢ Dark Gladiator

Technology: The Whirlwind Sword makes it possible to aim at numerous victims.

Sorcery Abilities: Present

- Knowledge

Diamond Blade: This blade makes it possible to aim at only one victim.

Growl Blade: This blade makes it possible to aim at only one victim.

Burning Blade: This blade makes it possible to aim at only one victim.

Frozen Blade: This blade makes it possible to aim at only one victim.

These fighting lessons are inclined to placing attacks than protecting against attacks. It is impossible for Duran to get any Gladiator armor but he has massive attack skills that allows him attack every opponent around.

When he uses sorcery with the blades, high injuries will be inflicted on enemies who have contradicting features. This is more effective when your team has a game persona well skilled in fighting without magic.

Second Lesson Adjustment

➢ Light/Light: White Knight

Necessary Materials: White Knight's Badge

Technology: The light flash sabre allows numerous victims to be aimed.

Sorcery Abilities:

- Beginnings

Heal Light: This spell makes it possible to aim at only one victim.

- Knowledge

Saint Blade: This blade makes it possible to aim at only one victim.

White Knight lessons dwell on both attacking and protection against attacks. The White Knight is able to use armors for protection and set off Heal Light. The White Knight gets familiar with the Saint Blade alongside strong aims on many victims. This blade affects ugly creatures that work in the Dark and this is a great asset for the concluding part of the game.

> Light/Dark: Baron

Necessary Materials: Baron's badge

Technology: The Magic Circle invention allows one on victim to be your aim.

Sorcery Abilities:

- Boosts

Heal Light: This allows you to choose to aim at just one victim or many victims.

Tinkle Rain: This allows you to aim only one victim.

The Baron has the ability to set off Heal Light on every character fighting on your side. A wise thing you can do is to transform your Duran to a Baron where your team does not include Carlie.

In a case where your team includes Carlie, taking this lesson is not really necessary as there is no other special thing about him apart from the Heal Light.

> Dark/Light: Sword fighter

Necessary Material: Sword fighter's badge

Technology: The Vacuum Sword invention allows you to aim at many victims.

Sorcery Abilities: Present

- Boosts

Diamond Blade: This blade makes it possible to aim at one or more opponents.

Growl Blade: This blade makes it possible to aim at one or more opponents.

Burning Blade: This blade makes it possible to aim at one or more opponents.

Frozen Blade: This blade makes it possible to aim at one or more opponents.

- Knowledge

Moon Blade: This blade makes it possible to aim at only one opponent.

Leaf Blade: This blade makes it possible to aim at only one opponent.

The sword fighter is able to engage in all blade sorceries available. He is however not allowed to use the Saint Blade and Dark Blade.

The Moon Blade empowers you to battle and not require constant restoration of health. The Leaf Blade serves as an instrument for preventing low MP for your game persona and achieving even when you do not have costly materials. In contrast with the offense abilities which do not have the potency of the Duelist, the sword fighter's sorcery abilities are most potent.

- ➢ Dark/Dark: Duelist

Necessary Material: Duelist's Badge

Technology: The Eruption Sword invention allows you to aim at many victims.

Sorcery Abilities:

- Beginning

Diamond Blade: This blade makes it possible to aim at only one victim.

Growl Blade: This blade makes it possible to aim at only one victim.

Burning Blade: This blade makes it possible to aim at only one victim.

Frozen Blade: This blade makes it possible to aim at only one victim.

- Knowledge

Dark Blade: This blade makes it possible to aim at only one victim.

In all Duran's lessons, the Duelist turns out as the one with the most strength to lead offense in battles. The Duelist possesses the Eruption Sword that be safely referred to as the technology with the highest potency throughout the game. However, the Duelist has the flaw of being able to get knowledge on just one sorcery skill, which is the Dark Blade that cannot be utilized when it is his turn.

Summary table [edit]

LIGHT	Fighter			DARK
	Tech: cross slash			
	Spell: *(none)*			
	Knight		Gladiator	
	Tech: Three step cut (S)		Tech: Whirlwind sword (M)	
	Spell: Heal light (S)		Spells: Diamond saber (S) Thunder saber (S) Flame saber (S) Ice saber (S)	
Paladin	Lord	Swordmaster	Duelist
Tech: Light flash blade (M)	Tech: Magic circle (S)	Tech: Vacuum sword (M)	Tech: Eruption sword (M)
Spell: Saint saber (S)	Spells: Tinkle rain (S)	Spells: Moon saber (S) Leaf saber (S)	Spell: Dark saber (S)
-	Upgraded: Heal light (M)	Upgraded: Ice saber (M) Thunder saber (M) Flame saber (M) Diamond saber (M)	-

❖ Hawk

Hawk is the fastest warrior that the game has. Although his strikes might not be as powerful as Duran's strikes, Hawk has the advantage of releasing the strikes two times quicker.

With this speed, Hawk is able to sharpen his skills again without taking so long. There are no lessons for him on sorcery in his early tutorials but he will be introduced to so many sorcery skills that are fun in his consequent tutorials.

> Beginning Lesson: Robbery

Skill: Falseness

Sorcery Ability: None

There are no sorcery abilities accessible to him. However, he makes up for this with his ability to give out really fast strikes.

Foremost Lesson Adjustment

> Light: Close Fighter

Technology: The Flying Swallow Toss invention makes it possible to aim at numerous victims.

Sorcery Abilities:

- Knowledge

Arrow: The arrow allows you to aim at only one victim.

Spike: The spear allows you to aim at only one victim.

Body Change: This allows you to aim at only one victim.

Sleep Flower: This allows you to aim at only one victim.

The Ranger has the skill to attack many opponents at the same time. The sad news about this is that the tutorials he will take part in later lack the skill to attack many opponents at a time.

Although the Body Change sorcery renders the opponent unusually small and powerless, it lets them earn no experience points at all, which is quite sad. This can still pass for a reasonable magic when there is an urgent situation.

Sleep Flower helps you take charge of many opponents' teams.

- Dark: Ninja

Technology: The Silhouette Slice invention allows you to aim at only one victim.

Sorcery Skills:

- Knowledge

Shuriken: This allows you to aim at only one victim. It also inflicts destruction and reduces the frequency with which attacks are received from opponents.

Flame Jutsu: This allows you to aim at only one victim. It also inflicts destruction and reduces the opponent's spell potency to both strike you and protect themselves from your strikes.

Aqua Jutsu: This allows you to aim at only one victim. It also inflicts destruction and reduces ability of the opponent to strike you.

Ground Jitsu: This allows you to aim at only one victim. It also inflicts destruction and reduces the ability of the opponent to dodge your attacks and the frequency with which attacks are received from opponents.

Growl Jutsu: This allows you to aim at only one victim.

It also inflicts destruction and reduces the ability of the opponents to protect themselves from your strikes.

The Ninja tutorial features several Jitsu magic with ability to reduce the skills of your opponents. You can utilize this effectively to finish off the leaders early or have more shields against them.

Alternate Lesson Adjustment

- Light/Light: Roamer.

Necessary Material: Die to attract Good Luck.

Skill: The Dance of Roses skill allows you to aim at only one victim.

Sorcery Ability: Present

- Beginning

Arrow: The arrow allows you to aim at only one victim.

Spike: The spear allows you to aim at only one victim.

- Boosts

Body Change: This allows you to aim at one or more victims.

Sleep Flower: This allows you to aim at one or more victims.

- Knowledge

Strength Top Up: This allows you to aim at only one victim.

Atmosphere Flutter: This allows you to aim at only one victim.

Poison Bubble: This allows you to aim at only one victim.

Semi Invisible: This allows you to aim at only one victim.

Psychotic: This allows you to aim at only one victim.

Life Top Up: This allows you to aim at only one victim.

Shape Shifter: This allows you to aim at only one victim.

Defense Spells: This allows you to aim at only one victim.

The roamer is able to make several achievements as he gains knowledge on nearly every Luna and Dryad magic available in the game. An insight into what the roamer can achieve is that he is able to top up the life of his associates as well as reduce the enemies' max HP to make them insane. A good strategy when using this is to open up with this when in a battle with a boss.

The roamer has the Counter Magic that makes him able to present his associates with armor to avoid destructive magic from the opponents. This spell works well when dealing with certain leaders and turns your fight against Koren into a walk-away one.

Poison Bubble inflicts destruction on your opponents and returns an amount of MP to Hawk. When Hawk collects this, he must maintain utmost caution so that he doesn't completely lose his ability to perform sorcery.

The flaws of the roamer are the less relevant nature of his sorcery skills.

Most of the sorcery skills cannot be used and some of them like the Energy boost are used only on extremely particular events.

In Hawk's concluding lessons, the roamer also possesses the least ability to sustain the offensive side in a battle.

> Light/Dark: Rouge

Necessary: Die to attract Bad and Luck

Skill: The Shadow Slash skill allows you to aim at only one victim.

Sorcery Abilities:

- Beginning

Arrow: The arrow allows you to aim at only one victim.

Spike: The spear allows you to aim at only one victim.

➢ Boosts

Body Change: This allows you to aim at one or more victims.

Sleep Flower: This allows you to aim at one or more victims.

- Knowledge

Rock Fall: The arrow allows you to aim at only one victim.

Land Mine: The arrow allows you to aim at only one victim.

Silver Dart: The arrow allows you to aim at only one victim.

Cutter Missile: The arrow allows you to aim at only one victim.

Axe Bomber: The arrow allows you to aim at only one victim.

Rocket Launcher: The arrow allows you to aim at only one victim.

Grenade Bomb: The arrow allows you to aim at only one victim.

Rogue's sorcery skills are mainly unique objects that can be easily flung.

The advantage of this comes in their ability to pause activity for a brief while since they have quite brief animation. Apart from the Pumpkin Bomb that makes Hawk have not just destruction infliction, but also MP, they majorly inflict destruction on their opponents.

The component of a strike and its potency are what makes one strike unique from the other. An example is the Silver Dart that is less potent yet its Holy component makes it possible for the Silver Dart to inflict destruction on ugly creatures you will encounter towards the game's conclusion.

It is possible to utilize the Pumpkin Bomb to make Hawk's usage of his sorcery go on for as long as possible but it needs you to employ extra caution. The only thing you can consider a disadvantage about the Rogue is the inability of his sorcery to destroy more than one enemy.

- Dark/Light: Ninja Master

Necessary Material: Bullseye Die

Skill: The Shadow Dive skill allows you to aim at only one victim.

Sorcery Abilities:

- Boosts

Shuriken: This allows you to aim at one or more victims.

Flame Jutsu: This allows you to aim at one or more victims.

Aqua Jutsu: This allows you to aim at one or more victims.

Ground Jutsu: This allows you to aim at one or more victims.

Growl Jutsu: This allows you to aim at one or more victims.

The Ninja Master gains knowledge on using the Ninja sorcery powers to destroy as many opponents as possible. This is most helpful during a battle with many strong enemies at the same time. Take battling with a set of Dark Lords as an instance, hitting every single enemy with the Water Jutsu reduces the potency of their Eruption Sword strike.

The Ninja Master is similar to the Nightblade where both of them have strength in playing the offensive.

- Dark/Dark: Nightblade

Necessary Material: Nighteye Die

Skill: The Split-Image Slice skill allows you to aim at only one victim.

Sorcery Ability:

- Beginning

Shuriken: This allows you to aim at only one victim.

Flame Jutsu: This allows you to aim at only one victim.

Aqua Jutsu: This allows you to aim at only one victim.

Ground Jutsu: This allows you to aim at only one victim.

Growl Jutsu: This allows you to aim at only one victim.

- Knowledge

Blow Needle: This allows you to aim at only one victim

Fire Breath: This allows you to aim at only one victim

Poison Breath: This allows you to aim at only one victim.

Deadly Weapon: This allows you to aim at only one victim. It inflicts destruction and reduces the opponent's max HP. This weapon comes in handy when battling with leaders.

Black Rain: This allows you to aim at more than one victim.

The Nightblade is a high level that has the advantage of a highly potent skill to attack more than one opponent at the same time. With Hawk's ability to strike two times, it is possible for him to boost this skill as fast as possible thereby increasing its functions.

The Nightblade is taught several sorcery abilities where some have more functions than the other.

The Fire Breath is a good example of the sorcery power with lesser functions. The Blow Needle shields you from the strong skills to attack many that your opponent might have by making the opponent go mute.

This mostly leads to ending the game and it does not matter that your life battery might be almost complete.

One magic that can be very helpful when applied the right way is the Deadly Weapon. It inflicts destruction of more than 999 by reducing the opponent's max HP by as much as 20%. You can use this in the beginning of a battle against a leader.

You must know that the Fire Breath has its imperfections. It has the ability to revoke all the sicknesses of your opponents. This means that any opponent that was affected by the Blow Needle gets unmated when Fire Breath comes in.

It seems like it is under some kind of external control since the burn sickness is still available in the game.

Still, it has been structured to have no adverse power which makes it only possible to erase any prior ailments using its burn ability that cannot inflict injury.

Summary table [edit]

LIGHT					DARK
	Thief				
	Tech: Backstab				
	Spell: *(none)*				
	Ranger			Ninja	
	Tech: Flying swallow toss (M)			Tech: Silhouette slice (S)	
	Spells: Arrow (S) Spike (S) Body change (S) Sleep flower (S)			Spells: Shuriken (S) Fire jutsu (S) Water jutsu (S) Earth jutsu (S) Thunder jutsu (S)	
	Wanderer	Rogue	Ninja Master		Nightblade
	Tech: Dance of roses (S)	Tech: Shadow slash (S)	Tech: Shadow dive (S)		Tech: Split-image slice (M)
	Spell: Energy boost (S) Aura wave (S) Poison bubble (S) Half vanish (S) Lunatic (S) Life booster (S) Trans-shape (S) Counter magic (S)	Spells: Rock fall (S) Land mine (S) Silver dart (S) Cutter missile (S) Crescent (S) Axe bomber (S) Rocket launcher (S) Grenade bomb (S)	-		Spells: Blow needle (S) Fire breath (S) Poison breath (S) Deadly weapon (S) Black rain (M)
	Upgraded: Body change (M) Sleep flower (M)	Upgraded: Body change (M) Sleep flower (M)	Upgraded: Shuriken (M) Fire jutsu (M) Water jutsu (M) Earth jutsu (M) Thunder jutsu (M)		-

Trials of Mana/Kevin's lessons

It can be concluded that Kevin is the strongest melee striker throughout the game. Duran might have greater destruction with his sword throws than Kevin with his hands, yet Kevin's blows come two times with one of Duran's throws. His ability to transform to a werewolf when it gets dark increases the potency of his strikes.

Kevin does not have many magic powers available to him and this can be considered a flaw for him. He can only gain access to a maximum of three magic powers towards the conclusion of the game.

There is a second unique quality of Kevin: Every lesson he attends (except the Grappler) gives him the throw tech that allows him strike only one opponent at a time. As soon as the grade 2 or 3 technology is launched by Kevin, it decides, without external influence, to select his default technology or go for the throw tech. You might find this frustrating where you consider a particular tech more helpful for a situation and Kevin selects a different one.

> Beginning Lesson: Grappler

Shape Shift: Werewolf

Technology: Ashura Dream Fist

The chance to have tutorials in magic is not available to him till his foremost lesson adjustment is completed.

Foremost Lesson Adjustment

> Light: Monk

Shape Shift: (Not available in English language)

Technology: The Whirlwind Kick technology allows you to aim at more than one victim.

Fling: Tornado Throw

Sorcery Abilities:

- Knowledge

Heal Light: This allows you to aim at only one victim.

Pressure Point: Personal

The Monk lesson cuts across several subjects. The Monk, who has the skill to strike many opponents at a time, is taught to use the Heal Light to make up for the absence of Carlie in your team.

The Monk is also taught to use the Pressure Point sorcery when battling with leaders in daytime. This gives him an almost equal or exactly equal strength as when he fights as a werewolf.

> Dark: Bashkar

Shape Shift: Black Fang

Technology: The Water-Moon Slice invention allows you to aim at only one victim.

Fling: Bastard Slam

Every other character except the Bashkar acquires sorcery knowledge in the second stage lesson.

However, Bashkar's great physical power is an equal substitution for the absent sorcery power.

Second Lesson Adjustment

- Light/Light: God Hand

Necessary Material: Gold Wolf Soul

Shape Shift: Gold Wolf

Technology: The Byakko Shock Wave technology allows you to aim at more than one victim.

Fling: Stardust Bomb

Sorcery Ability:

- Beginning

Heal Light: This allows you to aim at only one victim.

Pressure Point: Personal

- Knowledge:

Aura Wave: This allows you to aim at only one victim.

Apart from having a technology that lets you strike more than one opponent at a time, the God Hand also comes with an amazing sorcery ability which is the Aura Wave. This magic power instantly tops up the tech capacity of an associate right to its brim. This can also be applied to effect massive destruction on self or the Duelist, Nightblade or Swordmaster.

- Light/Dark: Fighting Monk

Necessary Material: Silver Wolf Soul

Shape Shift: Silver Wolf

Technology: The Genbu 100 Kick technology allows you to aim at only one victim.

Fling: Punch Impact

Sorcery Abilities:

- Beginning

Pressure Point: Personal

- Upgrades

Heal Light: This allows you to aim at one or more victims.

- Knowledge

Leaf Blade: This allows you to aim at only one victim.

The Fighting Monk is helpful with his healing powers as he is able to set off the Heal Light over all members of the group at the same time.

The Fighting Monk's healing ability comes in handy in the absence of Carlie as a member of your team.

He is able to prevent a low MP for all members of the group with his Leaf Blade.

The Fighting Monk has the least offense strength in all Kevin's last lessons yet he is still strong enough. His ability to aim at many enemies at a time comes as an advantage as there will be no clash of technology choices to use.

> Dark/Light: Death Hand

Necessary Material: Death Wolf Soul

Shape shift: Wolf Devil

Technology: The Seiryyu Death Fist technology allows you to aim at more than one victim.

Fling: Dead Crush

Sorcery Abilities:

- Knowledge

Energy Ball: This allows you to aim at only one victim. Death hand comes with the most offense potency in all Kevin's lessons.

The Energy Ball is used to boost serious strike opportunities but they are flawed and cannot give any achievement.

➢ Dark/Dark: Dervish

Necessary Material: Demon Wolf Soul

Shape Shift: Bloody Wolf

Technology: The Suzaku Sky Dance technology allows you to aim at more than one victim.

Fling: Veritubach

Sorcery Abilities:

- Knowledge

Moon Blade: This allows you to aim at only one victim.

Although it is very strong, the Death Hand comes with more offense strength than the Dervish. However, the Moon Blade comes before the Energy Ball in the area of helpfulness. The Moon Blade helps to regulate the need for constant health restoration while fighting.

Summary table [edit]

LIGHT				DARK
	Grappler			
	Night: Werewolf			
	Tech: Ashura dream fist			
	Spell: (none)			
	Monk		Bashkar	
	Night: ???		Night: Black fang	
	Tech: Whirlwind kick (M) Tornado throw		Tech: Water-moon slice (S) Bastard slam	
	Spells: Heal light (S) Pressure point (S)		Spells: (none)	
God hand	Warrior monk	Death hand	Dervish
Night: Gold wolf	Night: Silver wolf	Night: Wolf devil	Night: Bloody wolf
Tech: Byakko shock wave (M) Stardust bomb	Tech: Genbu 100 kick (S) Blow impact	Tech: Seiryuu death fist (M) Dead crush	Tech: Suzaku sky dance (M) Veritubach
Spell: Aura wave (S)	Spell: Leaf saber (S)	Spell: Energy ball (S)	Spell: Moon saber (S)
-	Upgraded: Heal light (M)	-	-

Trials of Mana/Angela's Lessons

Angela's strong destructive magic powers cover up for her low physical strength. Every sorcery abilities available to her can effect destruction. Still, only a number of Rune's Master's magic can achieve status effect alongside destruction.

Selecting Angela when you want a quick moving game can frustrate you since you will be forced to view her magic cartoons every now and then. You can also find them helpful if you employ the components that the ugly creatures do not have power over.

> ➢ Beginning Lesson: Sorcerer

Technology: Double Attack

Sorcery Abilities: Present

- Knowledge

Holy Ball: This has 2 MP that allows you to aim at one or more victims. It inflicts destruction with the holy component.

Gem Missile: This has 2 MP that allows you to aim at one or more victims. It inflicts destruction with the earth component.

Air Blast: This has 2 MP that allows you to aim at one or more victims. It inflicts destruction with the wind or thunder component.

Evil Gate: This has 2 MP that allows you to aim at one or more victims. It inflicts destruction with the dark component.

Ice Smash: This has 2 MP that allows you to aim at one or more victims. It inflicts destruction with the ice or water component.

Fireball: This has 2 MP that allows you to aim at one or more victims. It inflicts destruction with the fire component.

Angela is able to aim at every opponent at the same time with the vast knowledge she gains in sorcery. This does not change the fact that has low bodily strength to strike an opponent.

If you decide to alter Angela's lessons when she is yet to gain every sorcery skill, the skills will be moved to her new lesson when you get the adequate Spirit to continue.

Foremost Lesson Adjustment

> Light: Female Magician

Technology: The Pink Typhoon technology allows you to aim only one victim.

Sorcery Abilities: Present

- Beginning

Holy Ball: This has 2 MP that allows you to aim at one or more victims. It inflicts destruction with the holy component.

Gem Missile: This has 2 MP that allows you to aim at one or more victims. It inflicts destruction with the earth component.

Air Blast: This has 2 MP that allows you to aim at one or more victims. It inflicts destruction with the wind or thunder component.

Evil Gate: This has 2 MP that allows you to aim at one or more victims. It inflicts destruction with the dark component.

Ice Smash: This has 2 MP that allows you to aim at one or more victims. It inflicts destruction with the ice or water component.

Fireball: This has 2 MP that allows you to aim at one or more victims. It inflicts destruction with the fire component.

- Knowledge

Saint Beam: This has 5 MP that allows you to aim at one or more victims. It inflicts massive destruction with the holy component.

Earthquake: This has 4 MP that allows you to aim at one or more victims. It inflicts massive destruction with the earth component.

Thunderstorm: This has 4 MP that allows you to aim at one or more victims. It inflicts massive destruction with the wind or thunder component.

Mega Splash: This has 4 MP that allows you to aim at one or more victims. It inflicts massive destruction with the ice and water component.

Explode: This has 4 MP that allows you to aim at one or more victims. It inflicts massive destruction with the fire component.

The sorceress will be able to battle with some of the Godbeasts with some of the sorcery skills of higher grade that she is taught here. Those sorcery skills help her to stay in a hidden place and shoot alone opponents who are not strong to certain components.

Higher level sorcery skills will not be able to take down many opponents at a time until later in the game.

- Dark: Delvar

Technology: The Star Attack technology allows you to aim at only one victim.

Sorcery Abilities: Present

- Beginning

Holy Ball: This has 2 MP that allows you to aim at one or more victims. It inflicts destruction with the holy component.

Gem Missile: This has 2 MP that allows you to aim at one or more victims. It inflicts destruction with the earth component.

Air Blast: This has 2 MP that allows you to aim at one or more victims. It inflicts destruction with the wind or thunder component.

Evil Gate: This has 2 MP that allows you to aim at one or more victims. It inflicts destruction with the dark component.

Ice Smash: This has 2 MP that allows you to aim at one or more victims. It inflicts destruction with the ice or water component.

Fireball: This has 2 MP that allows you to aim at one or more victims. It inflicts destruction with the fire component.

- Knowledge

Dark Force: This has 5 MP that allows you to aim at only one victim. It inflicts massive destruction with the dark component.

Second Lesson Adjustment

> Light/Light: Grand Devina

Necessary Material: Arcane or Arcana Book

Technology: The Spiral Rod technology allows you to aim at only one victim.

Sorcery Abilities:

- Beginning

Holy Ball: This has 2 MP that allows you to aim at one or more victims. It inflicts destruction with the holy component.

Gem Missile: This has 2 MP that allows you to aim at one or more victims. It inflicts destruction with the earth component.

Air Blast: This has 2 MP that allows you to aim at one or more victims. It inflicts destruction with the wind or thunder component.

Evil Gate: This has 2 MP that allows you to aim at one or more victims. It inflicts destruction with the dark component.

Ice Smash: This has 2 MP that allows you to aim at one or more victims. It inflicts destruction with the ice or water component.

Fireball: This has 2 MP that allows you to aim at one or more victims. It inflicts destruction with the fire component.

- Boosts

Saint Beam: This has 5 MP that allows you to aim at one or more victims. It inflicts massive destruction with the holy component.

Earthquake: This has 4 MP that allows you to aim at one or more victims. It inflicts massive destruction with the earth component.

Thunderstorm: This has 4 MP that allows you to aim at one or more victims. It inflicts massive destruction with the wind or thunder component.

Mega Splash: This has 4 MP that allows you to aim at one or more victims. It inflicts massive destruction with the ice and water component.

Explode: This has 4 MP that allows you to aim at one or more victims. It inflicts massive destruction with the fire component.

- Knowledge

Double Spell: This has 9 MP that allows you to aim at many opponents. It inflicts massive destruction without any component.

The Grand Devina can be considered as almost the same with the Arch Mage. The point where Grand Devina is taught Double Spell and Arch Mage is taught Rainbow is the only thing that sets them apart. These two sorcery skills are highly potent and do not make use of ay component to strike every opponent at the same time.

However, in the area of physical and brain power, the Grand Devina tops the Arch Mage who tops him with a more advanced Spirit.

> Light/Dark: Arch Mage

Necessary Material: Esotera Book (Book of Secrets)

Technology: The Dancing Rod technology allows you to aim at only one victim.

Sorcery Abilities: Present

Holy Ball: This has 2 MP that allows you to aim at one or more victims. It inflicts destruction with the holy component.

Gem Missile: This has 2 MP that allows you to aim at one or more victims. It inflicts destruction with the earth component.

Air Blast: This has 2 MP that allows you to aim at one or more victims. It inflicts destruction with the wind or thunder component.

Evil Gate: This has 2 MP that allows you to aim at one or more victims. It inflicts destruction with the dark component.

Ice Smash: This has 2 MP that allows you to aim at one or more victims. It inflicts destruction with the ice or water component.

Fireball: This has 2 MP that allows you to aim at one or more victims. It inflicts destruction with the fire component.

- Boosts

Saint Beam: This has 5 MP that allows you to aim at one or more victims. It inflicts massive destruction with the holy component.

Earthquake: This has 4 MP that allows you to aim at one or more victims. It inflicts massive destruction with the earth component.

Thunderstorm: This has 4 MP that allows you to aim at one or more victims. It inflicts massive destruction with the wind or thunder component.

Mega Splash: This has 4 MP that allows you to aim at one or more victims. It inflicts massive destruction with the ice and water component.

Explode: This has 4 MP that allows you to aim at one or more victims. It inflicts massive destruction with the fire component.

- Knowledge

Rainbow: This has 10 MP that allows you to aim at many opponents. It inflicts massive destruction without any component.

The Grand Devina can be considered as almost the same with the Arch Mage. The point where Grand

Devina is taught Double Spell and Arch Mage is taught Rainbow is the only thing that sets them apart.

These two sorcery skills are highly potent and do not make use of ay component to strike every opponent at the same time.

However, in the area of physical and brain power, the Grand Devina tops the Arch Mage who tops him with a more advanced Spirit.

> Dark/Light: Rune Master

Necessary Material: Book of Rune

Technology: The 1ot technology allows you to aim at only one victim.

Sorcery Abilities:

- Beginning

Holy Ball: This has 2 MP that allows you to aim at one or more victims. It inflicts destruction with the holy component.

Gem Missile: This has 2 MP that allows you to aim at one or more victims. It inflicts destruction with the earth component.

Air Blast: This has 2 MP that allows you to aim at one or more victims. It inflicts destruction with the wind or thunder component.

Evil Gate: This has 2 MP that allows you to aim at one or more victims. It inflicts destruction with the dark component.

Ice Smash: This has 2 MP that allows you to aim at one or more victims. It inflicts destruction with the ice or water component.

Fireball: This has 2 MP that allows you to aim at one or more victims. It inflicts destruction with the fire component.

- Boosts

Dark Force: This allows you to aim at one or more victims. It inflicts massive destruction with the dark component.

- Knowledge

Stone Cloud: This has 7 MP that allows you to aim at only one victim. It inflicts extremely massive destruction with the earth component and can change the opponent into stone after a while.

Stun Wind: This has 7 MP that allows you to aim at only one victim. It inflicts extremely massive destruction with the wind component and can make the enemy go mute.

Cold Breeze: This has 7 MP that allows you to aim at only one victim. It inflicts extremely massive destruction with the ice and changes the enemy to an ice figure.

Blaze Wall: This has 7 MP that allows you to aim at only one victim. It inflicts extremely massive destruction with the fire component and has no unique feature.

Death Spell: This has 8 MP that allows you to aim at only one victim. This makes any opponent who gets attacked to die instantly.

The Rune Master acquires the best sorcery skills that make use of components and allow it to aim at only one victim. There are three of these sorcery skills that create unique status effects on the opponent. The Rune Master therefore turns out to be a highly skilled shooter so long as the opponent in mind is has low resistance to a particular component.

You might experience difficulties with the expensive prices of MP especially when you are in a serious battle with a boss or in dark underground prisons.

The Death Spell comes as the strongest one-opponent sorcery skill as it effects as much as 999 destructions on the opponent whether there is a counter spell protection or it is a boss.

However, the Death Spell cannot affect the ugly creatures except you are equal to them or higher than them.

- Dark/Dark: Magus

Necessary Material: Forbidden Book

Technology: The Hot Shot technology allows you to aim at only one opponent.

Sorcery Skills:

- Beginning

Holy Ball: This has 2 MP that allows you to aim at one or more victims. It inflicts destruction with the holy component.

Gem Missile: This has 2 MP that allows you to aim at one or more victims. It inflicts destruction with the earth component.

Air Blast: This has 2 MP that allows you to aim at one or more victims. It inflicts destruction with the wind or thunder component.

Evil Gate: This has 2 MP that allows you to aim at one or more victims. It inflicts destruction with the dark component.

Ice Smash: This has 2 MP that allows you to aim at one or more victims. It inflicts destruction with the ice or water component.

Fireball: This has 2 MP that allows you to aim at one or more victims. It inflicts destruction with the fire component.

Dark Force: This has 5 MP that allows you to aim at only one victim. It inflicts massive destruction with the dark component.

- Knowledge

Earthquake: This has 4 MP that allows you to aim at only one victim.

Thunderstorm: This has 4 MP that allows you to aim at only one victim.

Mega Splash: This has 4 MP that allows you to aim at only one victim.

Explode: This has 4 MP that allows you to aim at only one victim.

Ancient: This has 12 MP that allows you to aim at many victims. It inflicts major destructions without any component.

The Magus turns out as the character with the most brain power in Angela's lessons. With this, she is able to achieve high number of destructions with less sophisticated sorcery skills above other lessons.

Although the strongest many-opponent sorcery skill is Ancient, its disadvantage is in its expensive MP price and high cartoon duration during the game. Also, when Magus is taught higher level sorcery skills, they fail to attain the stage of striking many opponents at a time.

LIGHT				DARK
	Magician			
	Tech: Double attack			
	Spells: Holy ball (M) Gem missile (M) Air blast (M) Evil gate (M) Ice smash (M) Fireball			

Sorceress		Delvar	
Tech: Pink typhoon (S)		Tech: Star attack (S)	
Spells: Saint beam (S) Earthquake (S) Thunderstorm (S) Mega splash (S) Explode (S)		Spells: Dark force (S)	

Grand Devina	Arch Mage	Rune Master	Magus
Tech: Spiral rod (S)	Tech: Dancing rod (S)	Tech: 10t (S)	Tech: Hot shot (S)
Spell: Double spell (M)	Spell: Rainbow (M)	Spells: Stone cloud (S) Stun wind (S) Cold breeze (S) Blaze wall (S) Deathspell (S)	Spells: Earthquake (S) Thunderstorm (S) Mega splash (S) Explode (S) Ancient (M)
Upgraded: Saint beam (M) Earthquake (M) Thunderstorm (M) Mega splash (M) Explode (M)	Upgraded: Saint beam (M) Earthquake (M) Thunderstorm (M) Mega splash (M) Explode (M)	Upgraded: Dark Force (M)	

Trials of Mana/Lise's Lessons

Lise strikes pretty well and gives good assists with the sorcery skills she has. Her last lessons include five sorcery skills, where one is summon that strikes every opponent in the area and the other for sorcery skills can lower or increase features of the opponents.

She has sorcery skills that can change the status of an opponent and works very well on leaders. Her summon has the ability to cause destruction and alter the status of the enemy.

- ➤ Beginning Lesson: Amazon

Technology: Whirlwind Lance

She is not eligible to be taught any sorcery skill till she undergoes her first lesson alteration. She is reasonably good in striking an offense.

Foremost Lesson Adjustment

- Light: Valkyrie

Technology: The Vacuum Surge Spear technology allows many victims.

- Knowledge

Speed Up: This allows you to aim at only one victim.

Protect Up: This allows you to aim at only one victim.

Mind Up: This allows you to aim at only one victim.

Power Up: This allows you to aim at only one victim.

Valkyrie will be your best option when you are looking for ways to boost the features of your associates. This comes as a plus for you as Lise is the only game persona that can receive lessons on every sorcery skills for assisting, unlike the Ninja Hawk and Witchy Carlie who only have access to sorcery skills that reduce features.

Combining Valkyrie with a game persona with disabling sorcery skills when fighting bosses will help you definitely perform exceptionally.

- Dark: Rune Maiden

Technology: The Flying Heaven Spear technology allows you to aim at many opponents.

Sorcery Skills: Present

- Knowledge

Speed Down: This allows you to aim at only one victim.

Protect Down: This allows you to aim at only one victim.

Mind Down: This allows you to aim at only one victim.

Power Down: This allows you to aim at only one victim.

The Rune Maiden should be your choice where your aim is to reduce the features of your opponents. Where the reducing skill needs only one set off to have effect, raising the features of every of your associates at a time need you to apply it thrice. This means that going for the reduction skill works better in boss fights.

Second Lesson Adjustment

> Light/Light: Vanadis

Necessary Material: Briesingamen

Technology: The Light Ball Spear technology allows you to aim at many opponents.

Sorcery Skills:

- Beginning

Speed Up: This allows you to aim at only one victim.

Protect Up: This allows you to aim at only one victim.

Mind Up: This allows you to aim at only one victim.

Power Up: This allows you to aim at only one victim.

- Knowledge

Freya: This allows you to aim at many opponents.

Vanadis' skill to strike many opponents at a time, along with her offense strength, outshines the rest in Lise's last lessons. She is able to reduce the size of the opponents and increases their vulnerability to death with her summon. This should only be used in last minute cases since you do not gain any experience from them.

Vanadis' flaw comes in the inability of her assist sorcery, like Star Lancer's to reach every of her associates at a time.

- Light/Dark: Star Lancer

Necessary Material: Morning Star Chain

Technology: The Flying Heaven Spear technology allows you to aim at only one opponent.

Sorcery Skills: Present

- Boosts

Speed Up: This allows you to aim at one or more victims.

Protect Up: This allows you to aim at one or more victims.

Mind Up: This allows you to aim at one or more victims.

Power Up: This allows you to aim at one or more victims.

- Knowledge

Marduk: This allows you to aim at many opponents.

The Star Lancer is able to cover every associate with the assist sorcery and get the team ready for a major battle with a boss.

She is also able to prevent opponents from giving their best strikes by muting them with the summon she has.

➢ Dark/Light: Dragon Master

Necessary Material: Knight Dragon Chain

Technology: The Dragon Fang Spear technology allows you to aim at only one opponent.

Sorcery Abilities:

Speed Down: This allows you to aim at only one victim.

Protect Down: This allows you to aim at only one victim.

Mind Down: This allows you to aim at only one victim.

Power Down: This allows you to aim at only one victim.

- Knowledge

Jormundgand: This allows you to aim at many victims.

The summon of the Dragon Master, which is the fastest to be taught and the fastest to set off, has the ability to make opponents take in deadly substances. She is not grounded on aiming at many opponents with her sorcery for reducing features. Still, there is no need to worry as it is difficult to find the ugly creatures that only a combination of Power and Mind Down can take down.

> Dark/Dark: Fenrir Knight

Necessary Material: Gleipnir

Technology: The Hundred Flower Dance allows you to aim at only one victim.

Sorcery Abilities: Present

> Boosts

Speed Down: This allows you to aim at one or more victims.

Protect Down: This allows you to aim at one or more victims.

Mind Down: This allows you to aim at one or more victims.

Power Down: This allows you to aim at one or more victims.

- Knowledge

Lamian Naga: This allows you to aim at many victims.

Lamian Naga is the summon of Fenrir Knight and the amount of destruction it inflicts is higher than whichever summon Lise is eligible to get lessons in.

Unfortunately, Lamian Naga is not able to produce status effect on an opponent. Another thing she is taught is battling many strong ugly creatures using her reduction sorcery skills to aim at all of them. A good instance is setting off sets of Nightblades with the Power Down. This reduces the potency of the opponent's Split-Image Slice.

Summary table [edit]

LIGHT					DARK
	Amazon				
	Tech: Whirlwind lance				
	Spells: *(none)*				
	Valkyrie		Rune Maiden		
	Tech: Vacuum surge spear (M)		Flying heaven spear (M)		
	Spells: Speed up (S) / Protect up (S) / Mind up (S) / Power up (S)		Spells: Speed down (S) / Protect down (S) / Mind down (S) / Power down (S)		
	Vanadis	Star Lancer	Dragon Master	Fenrir Knight	
	Tech: Light ball spear (M)	Tech: Morningstar chain (S)	Tech: Dragon Tooth Spear (S)	Tech: Hundred flowers dance (S)	
	Summon: Freya (M)	Summon: Marduk (M)	Summon: Jormundgand (M)	Summon: Lamian Naga (M)	
		Upgraded: Speed up (M) / Protect up (M) / Mind up (M) / Power up (M)		Upgraded: Speed down (M) / Protect down (M) / Mind down (M) / Power down (M)	

Trials of Mana/Carlie's Lessons

You do not have to rely on materials as Carlie is able to receive lessons on sorcery skills to restore health as soon as the game begins. In her various lessons, she is able to learn sorcery skills like Blade magic, Black Curse and many other sorceries that can cause destruction.

- ➢ Beginning Lesson: Male Priest

Technology: Blonke

Sorcery Skills: Present

- Knowledge

Heal Light: This allows you to aim at only one victim.

Tinkle Rain: This allows you to aim at only one victim.

She has low bodily offense strength and has no sorcery skill that can cause destruction. She proves helpful, albeit, as she turns out as the alone game persona who does not need to go through any lesson adjustment in order to restore health.

Foremost Lesson Adjustment

- Light: Female Clergy

Technology: The Jump technology allows you to aim at only one victim.

Sorcery Skills:

Tinkle Rain: This allows you to aim at only one victim.

- Boosts

Heal Light: This allows you to aim at one or more victims.

- Knowledge

Holy Ball: This allows you to aim at only one victim.

Diamond Blade: This allows you to aim at only one victim.

Thunder Blade: This allows you to aim at only one victim.

Flame Blade: This allows you to aim at only one victim.

Ice Blade: This allows you to aim at only one victim.

The Holy Ball skill which the female clergy acquires is able to inflict reasonable destruction on opponents who have Dark components. It might not be really helpful to set off self-Blade magic but they can prove potent if set off on stronger associates.

➢ Dark: Enchantress

Technology: The Dash technology allows you to aim at only one victim.

Sorcery Skill: Present

- Beginning

Tinkle Rain: This allows you to aim at only one victim.

- Boosts

Heal Light: This allows you to aim at one or more victims.

- Knowledge

Unicorn Head: This allows you to aim at only one victim.

Machine Golem: This allows you to aim at only one victim.

The Enchantress learns certain summon sorcery skills which brings ugly creatures to destroy an enemy. Although it might not be helpful like the Female Clergy's magic on ugly creatures with ice, fire, air or earth components, their performance is reasonable enough.

Second Lesson Adjustment

> Light/Light: Bishop

Necessary Material: Holy Bottle or Holy Water Vial

Technology: The Chop-Chop technology allows you to aim at only one victim.

Sorcery Abilities:

- Beginning

Heal Light: This allows you to aim at one or more victims.

Holy Ball: This allows you to aim at only one victim.

Diamond Blade: This allows you to aim at only one victim.

Thunder Blade: This allows you to aim at only one victim.

Flame Blade: This allows you to aim at only one victim.

Ice Blade: This allows you to aim at only one victim.

Boosts

Tinkle Rain: This allows you to aim at one or more victims.

- Knowledge

Saint Blade: This allows you to aim at only one victim.

Magic Protection: This allows you to aim at only one victim.

Turn Undead: This allows you to aim at many victims.

A lot of ugly creatures towards the conclusion of the game have dark components which makes the Saint Blade helpful. Turn Undead is quite cheap as you spend just 1 MP to achieve 999 total destructions on every undead ugly creature in the area as well as some bosses. You can really use this if you end up in the Mirage Palace under Carlie or Kevin's reign and it only affects undead ugly creatures that are not up to Carlie's stage.

> Light/Dark: Sage

Necessary Material: Salt Bottle or Bottle of Salt

Technology: The Boom-Boom technology allows you to aim at only one victim.

Sorcery Skills:

Heal Light: This allows you to aim at one or more victims.

- Boosts

Tinkle Rain: This allows you to aim at one or more victims.

Holy Ball: This allows you to aim at one or more victims.

Diamond Blade: This allows you to aim at one or more victims.

Thunder Blade: This allows you to aim at one or more victims.

Flame Blade: This allows you to aim at one or more victims.

Ice Blade: This allows you to aim at one or more victims.

- Knowledge

Saint Beam: This allows you to aim at only one victim.

The Sage gains skills in using the magic she acquired while a female clergy to attack many opponents at a time. It might as well be a waste of time since you might not consider the Holy Ball towards the conclusion of the game as it is not very strong. Also, it takes a lot of time to use Blade magic to attack many opponents at a time.

The Sage gets familiar with the Saint Beam magic that might be reasonable but has no uniqueness, especially as Angela is able to access it when she is a female magician and in the second stage lesson.

➢ Dark/Light: Sorceress

Necessary Material: Bottle of Ashes

Technology: The Crazy technology allows you to aim at only one victim.

Sorcery Abilities

Heal Light: This allows you to aim at one or more victims.

Unicorn Head: This allows you to aim at only one victim.

Machine Golem: This allows you to aim at only one victim.

- Boosts

Tinkle Rain: This allows you to aim at one or more victims.

- Knowledge

Ghoul: This allows you to aim at only one victim.

Ghost: This allows you to aim at only one victim.

Dark Blade: This allows you to aim at only one victim.

Black Curse: This allows you to aim at only one victim.

➢ Dark/Dark: Dark Shaman

Necessary Material: Bottle of Blood

Technology: The Huge-Huge technology allows you to aim at only one victim.

In the midst of several attributes, the Sorceress is taught the Black Curse which can assist in reducing every feature of the opponent. It can also work well on bosses as your destruction result increases and theirs decreases. She is taught certain magic that help her seek the undead to strike opponents.

Sorcery Abilities:

Heal Light: This allows you to aim at one or more victims.

Unicorn Head: This allows you to aim at only one victim.

Machine Golem: This allows you to aim at only one victim.

- Knowledge

Anti-Magic: This allows you to aim at only one victim.

Gremlin: This allows you to aim at only one victim.

Great Demon: This allows you to aim at only one victim.

Demon Breath: This allows you to aim at many victims.

In lessons on how to carry out the best attacks, Dark Shaman takes the lead. This is with the exception of a battle with the Undead where the Bishop leads the game. With Demon Breath, every enemy is broken and have protection sorcery reduced. The Greta Demon has the highest potency in all of Carlie's sorceries.

The books have proved Anti Magic to be helpful as it dissolves magic like Blade magic and star boost magic set off by an opponent. Still, it is not frequently employed as it is rare to find bosses who put the magic for their own use.

LIGHT	Cleric			DARK
	Tech: Bonkle			
	Spells: Heal Light (S) Tinkle Rain (S)			
	Priestess		Enchantress	
	Tech: Jump (S)		Dash (S)	
	Spells: Holy Ball (S) Diamond Saber (S) Thunder Saber (S) Flame Saber (S) Ice Saber (S)		Summon: Unicorn Head (S) Machine Golem (S)	
	Both Upgraded: Heal Light (M)			
	Bishop	Sage	Necromancer	Dark Shaman
	Tech: ChopChop (S)	Tech: BoomBoom (S)	Tech: Craaaazy (S)	Tech: HugeHuge (S)
	Summon: (None)	Summon: (None)	Summon: Ghoul (S) Ghost (S)	Summon: Gremlin (S) Great Demon (S)
	Spells: Saint Saber (S) Magic Shield (S) Turn Undead (M)	Spells: Saint Beam (S)	Spells: Dark Saber (S) Black Curse (S)	Spells: AntiMagic (S) Demon Breath (M)
	Upgraded: Tinkle Rain (M)	Upgraded: Tinkle Rain (M) Holy Ball (M) Diamond Saber (M) Thunder Saber (M) Flame Saber (M) Ice Saber (M)	Upgraded: Tinkle Rain (M)	-

Control

Control	Usage
✚	Move your character up, down, left, and right.
Ⓐ	Attack, talk or interact with people or objects, confirm menu selections, and progress dialogue.
Ⓑ	Use a technique, or cancel menu items.
Ⓧ	Display the item ring.
Ⓨ	Display menus.
START	Display storage.
SELECT	Switch characters. Also switches between characters in the menu, such as in the equipment screen.
L or R	When displaying the item ring, press to switch between character rings.

Trials of Mana/Part 1: The Legend of Mana

The fun is about to begin. Six game personas are presented to you and they are all casual people. They can only graduate to Mana's deliverers when they get teachings and then practical knowledge. Isn't this interesting?

You should not select any character until you have checked out details concerning all the characters. Your group members should spread equally across all personas you feel are interesting. You must also know that your different characters have different level of tough tasks towards the end of the game. Your choice of a head determines their task toughness.

The game personas have been split into different sections based on the difficulty of their last boss battle. This is to help you prevent you from having awful last battles.

Note: This toughness varies and the last bosses of Kevin and Carlie are very tough enemies.

Your group selection process, you should be focused on the potential toughness and flaws that are likely to come your way. If you do not have Carlie in your team, materials to restore health have to be purchased and your game could be a lot slow-paced and tougher. Carlie is definitely a good option especially for newbie players.

Either Kevin or Duran can be a good cover up for Carlie where purchasing materials at the beginning of the game is not a problem for you and your also prefer to finish up the ugly creatures speedily. These two game personas are skilled warriors and can gain knowledge on how to set off Heal Light on the entire team.

Well, this can only happen when they get in the appropriate lesson such as Duran as a Lord and Kevin as a Warrior Monk. This way, they can perfect their Heal Light just like Carlie towards the close of the game.

You should also be aware that placing Carlie as your third game persona will make her be a part of your group earlier than the actual position of the third game persona. To simply say, Carlie should be placed as your first game persona to enable her go through the entire game with you. Place her in the third if you prefer her to not be your first but bottom line is: Never place Carlie in the second place.

Angela

Angela is the black sheep of her family. She is the daughter of Valda, who is the queen of Altena. Altena is filled with high level sorcerers and witches but Angela has zero sorcery skills. Well, maybe not yet.

We should probably move over to Jose now.

Carlie

This is the point where you relax and enjoy the cut-scene. Carlie has no parents and is under the care of Heath. Heath is diviner whose entire hair is totally white. Carlie hides in a dark area to eavesdrop on a conversation between Heath and the old Priest of Light. They are discussing mysterious events in Mana.

You have to take a tour at the end of the cut-scene. You might want to know more about Wendel so you should speak with the NPCs. Return to Carlie's chamber as soon as you are done then walk over to the other room at the other side of the hallway. You will locate this room by going to the room that Carlie and Heath walked into each other and then locate the door by the left. Speak with him and then return to Carlie's room to get some rest.

It is currently after dark so you are free to walk out of the house and make fun of NPCs who cannot sleep before going down to the deck. You might not see it on time so go to Carlie's room and turn south.

Walk down to the exit by the right so you can reach the ledge.

Mickbrings up a banekujako. Although the Japanese that I have might not be extremely peculiar, it is a beautiful yellow spring. When you climb on it, it gives you access to leave the sanctuary to go to a spectacular beauty style.

You will have a tumble embarrassingly over a game persona who is to join you in short while. You will be lead to Astoria by this character. Do not forget the exact place of your landing as that is the way to get into the Cave of Waterfalls.

You are free to continue going when you have had a brief conversation. You are to walk towards the north and experience battling against the Rabites. You only have to press A to get them slammed. The succeeding phase will teach you skills to use more potent strikes when in a battle. Keep to the north till you see Heath. The cut scene is easy to understand, what you have to do is pay attention to the three sorcery cartoons, Holy Ball, Back Curse and Evil Gate, as they come up.

They are bound to come up a second time while Carlie is free to visit a place at the end of the street to be taught the Black Curse.

When this is over, the names of characters will be shown. You can now move on to another chapter in the guide.

Duran

A competition venue where Buiser, the last enemy, sits close to you is the place where Duran kicks off his adventure. Maintain the A strike till the colour of the gauge at the end of the page turns screen. Now, simply hit B and he will be thrown off to land on his back. He is a cheap opponent so your victory against him is assured. Your death in his hands is not a big deal since you get your total healing immediately. When your battle is over and you have won, you will be complimented by King Richard.

This is the point where an interesting and engaging cut-scene filled with lots of information comes up. You should capture Loki's face in your mind and listen well as he speaks on the Dragon Emperor.

You are definitely going to meet Loki another time within the game.

Someone will kill some of the security men and leave some others with terrible wounds while you are asleep. When you get up and speak to the security man closest to you, the criminal will show up. He will be clad in red so you have to trail him. He is going to appear to you as a sorcerer and will not go straight to attacking you with Fireball and Ice Smash; he will get friendly with you. Keep up with the cut-scene till you are back in charge.

Apparently, Duran loves to take alcoholic wine but you are to go out of the café and take the north way to the house close to you. When you go up the staircase, you will find a door that will lead you to a soothsayer.

You will be told by the soothsayer to get to Wendel. She will also advise you that taking lesson adjustments have the possibility of increasing your strength. When you leave there, take the corner to the southeast that has an interlocking with the armor and weapons store. That route will lead you to where Duran leaves.

Climb the stairs to get to Duran's chamber and uncover the treasure box. You can now go out of his home.

In the following half a minute, you will watch scenes that can make you cry. You cannot move out without speaking with King Richard. You will find him by maintaining the way down the several north roads you will pass until you meet him. When the meeting is over, keep to the south and the east till you get to a place that the Earth divides. Go to the other side with the help of the bridge before finding a place to relax and view the character appreciation.

Hawk

Relax and view how the robbers run along Sand City Sultan. You become in charge as soon as Hawk walks into the room then uncover the treasure box to hurl insulting words at the businessman before hopping out through the door of the terrace. The cut-scene will keep going on.

After the cur-scene, your tourism of the land begins.

It is necessary for you to go round the area and discover places since the game will lead you to this place again later on. Away from that, you have to know where Eagle is. In order to get to his room which is last room east of the castle, you will take the way that leads across the terrace.

Finding Eagle when you get to his house will be easy since he will be moving back and forth in his room. Walk up to him in his room and speak with him and watch him rush furiously to Flamekhan's chamber when you have reached a common ground with him. You are to join him in Flamekhan's chamber which is on the right side of the throne chamber.

Isabella and the mysterious fellow who looks like a vampire will have a conversation before she engages in a battle with Eagle. There is no need to panic since pressing A will only make him exhausted to give you your victory rather than leave him dead. This is where Isabella comes in to strike him with the Fireball to cause his final death. The cut-scene continues.

You might feel frustrated when you discover you have fallen into a set up. Make a hole through the prison bar or the wall behind to lead to the occurrence of certain events. Move out of Navarre and avoid dying in the hands of Ninjas when Nikita helps you escape.

Enjoy the cut-scene appreciation and let the discovery that your encounters were all predetermined serve as a comic relief for you.

Kevin

A number of cut-scenes that feature the treaty between the Beast King and the Deathjester will be the starting point of Kevin's journey. The next thing is a brief cut-scene where Kevin and Karl are in a bush. Karl is Kevin's pet wolf. You will be coerced into a battle with a Karl who comes up as mean, which is quite unusual.

You have the options of using A button to achieve common blows and strikes or to join the B button with a complete bar. The latter option functions with the original button settings. Since Karl is not necessarily weak, there is a possibility that you will get into a defenceless situation. Anyway, Kevin is a mini human and mini beast and there is the suspicion that they encounter mysterious things in the dark.

The battle with your closest pal is over and you have won so you begin to cry in extreme pain. When you have walked aimlessly in the bush for a while, the game switches to the castle in Beast Kingdom. Here, you can move around freely and engage other Beastmen in conversations.

When you go out of the castle, you win run into the king and the Deathjester's secret discussion which will reveal to you that they should be held accountable for Karl's strange acts. An angry Kevin breaks a hole in a wall to challenge the Beast King. Unfortunately, he is no match for the Beast King.

When you wake up in the bush, you can choose to take a walk to the statue of Mana made in gold. It is a short distance from where you are. You will see Deathjester roaming a closed path and Kevin is angry and seeks to retaliate over the killing of his pet wolf.

However, Deathjester begins a narrative that includes Wendel. He agrees to visit the place but not out of his freewill.

Lise

Lise's journey starts where she is teaching her trainees ways to win in a fight against a pink bird. Hitting the A tab will strike and hitting the B tab will release a unique strike as the gauge to the end gets full and changes to green. Although the bird is high in HP, death should be your least of concerns. However, in the worst scenario where you die, your trainees simply need to boost your gaiety and you will be restored.

When you have killed the bird, a cut-scene will appear and Lise will be under your care. Turn north to the throne chamber and go ahead to have a word with the king. After that, take the door towards the corner that is northeast of the chamber and use the stairs to reach down the corner that is southeast of the chamber.

A chamber with large breadth will be opened up to you so you have to reach the end of the room on the east and turn north so you can speak with the security man by the door. Take the same stairs you took to get here that is on the extreme end of the chamber by the west and leads to the south of the north. There are two doors new chamber you have entered and both of them will take you north-way. Take the door by your right and approach the old woman you see in the chamber.

A new cut-scene exposing Lise's early life and where Elliot presently lives will come up.

As soon as Lise returns to your charge, return north and walk into the chamber of the king. You will see two staircases and one leads southeast of the king and the southwest of the king. Take any staircase you prefer as they have the same destination and take same route down south and you will come out of the palace.

Turn east and then try to remember the exact place Elliot was in the cut-scene. Head to the south, walk into the entrance by the west then restore health and store with the goddess figure. Take the door at the end of the stairs and finally meet Elliot.

Sadly, the ninja arrives earlier than you to carry out his malicious scheme. Lise is also impatient because she has to meet up with the king so she abandons Elliot.

Return to the king's chamber after Lise returns to your charge. Just in case you have forgotten the way back, take the south door and keep west till you get to a large entrance which you will enter and continue north.

Don't forget to annihilate every ninja you come across with. There is no need to attempt returning to pick Elliot since the ninjas will have disappeared alongside him when you get there.

Some cut-scenes will show followed by character appreciation when you arrive at the throne chamber.

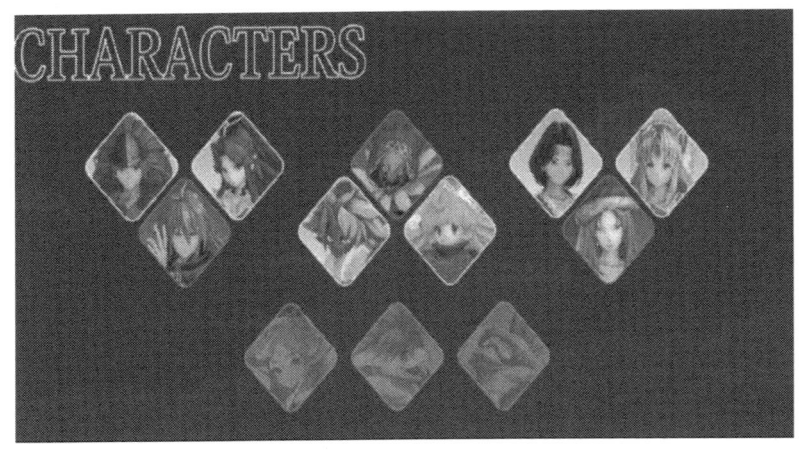

Trials of Mana/Part 2: The Mana Fairy

When the chamber appreciation ends, your play session begins in any of the two venues. Your first appearance as Carlie is in the Lakeshore Village Astoria and this means you can walk over the part of this guide that covers the Castle City Jad. The first appearance of the rest game personas is in the Castle City Jad from where they go on to the Lakeshore Village.

> **Castle City Jad**

The beastmen rule this town and cannot let you go out of the town. You should not think about purchasing arms from traders as the beastmen have seized them as the town's property. You are alone at this point as none of the game personas you selected will be able to come in yet. Although you will encounter four game personas (they do not include) while exploring the town, it is impossible for them to play the game.

The good news is that there is a way to escape the town when it is dark. The beastmen are probably keeping you back so they can kill you after they have transformed. What you need to do is to remain at the guesthouse and ask the landlord to call you from your sleep when it gets dark. Take your south as you come out of the guesthouse and destroy all Bound Wolves you come across on your way. Keep to your south and ensure to annihilate the Myconids and Rabites you meet till you get to Lakeshore Village Astoria.

> **Lakeshore Village Astoria**

You have arrived in Lakeshore Village Astoria and this is going to be a short stay for you. The first thing you have to do is to speak with two NPCs else the game remains at a standpoint. One of the NPCs is a woman on the east end who will inform you that you just have to cross the pool of water to get to Wendel. The other NPC is a man on the south end that delights in telling tales of strange battles.

Your next stop should be the arms store where you will purchase fresh arms. In order to get your new arms fortified, Click the Y tab to reveal a list and scroll to the equipment segment at the top right end and select the A tab.

A control icon will come up so you have to click on A tab a second time to select the arms you want. Direct your control icon to the arms you have selected and click on A tab. You have gotten familiar with switching the weapons of your game persona so trade off the old arms and return to the guesthouse to get some rest. Or, you can walk to the bush to boost your grade. This is totally your choice to make.

A sharp illumination will startle you up from your nap and you have to trace it down to the bush. This part is not complicated. All you have to do is go through the Cave of Waterfalls route then go left and maintain the path till you get to the Golden Goddess Statue.

There are similar statues spread over the universe and they are all pictures of what the Mana Goddess looks like. They are powerful as the statues made of gold can revive your MP and HP. You will be able to store your play session with the gold as well as the silver statues. That is your next task.

Keep up with that route till a new scene comes up, revealing a strange statue on the roof a building.

It does not have the power to cause any harm yet but ensure to remember the exact place it is located for future purposes. Continue down the path till you get to the light. At the close of this part, you will have a Mana Fairy placed in your head.

The game persona you have will determine whether conceit or fright will be caused by the fairy. You can now return to Astoria.

It is surely tragic to meet Astoria in ashes and you can choose to mourn the land but you have to return to the bush to get learn primary things about battles in Trials of Mana. Otherwise, move to the new section.

The Art of Killing Rabites

The heads-up display

You will see the heads-up display at the end of the page, so recognize all the components included. To the top is the HP which is the large group of numbers, to the left is the amount of HP remaining, to the right is the total HP and down is the picture of your game persona.

There will be an alteration in this when status effects come in. Anytime Kevin changes form, his picture switches to that of the werewolf. On the left, the LV represents level and on the right is the outstanding MP.

The bands around the pictures of your game personas signify their techniques and they glow in blue color with each offense you give. A technique is available for your use if the bands turn green or red or yellow.

You must get familiar with your with your techniques before rushing off to the bush to look for Rabites. Rabites possess 20 HP and that is just about the right number we require. Strike your opponent four times with the A Button-button and give a little time before you carry out another offense.

The game controls the time between the first and the second strike as you can only strike again when the arms of your game persona gets very bright and the technique band starts to shine in green color. At this point, you can hit the B tab and the game persona starts to shine in white and sparkles of light all over. The game persona will start to make strange sounds and you will see that your game persona is having an epileptic attack. You don't have to get tensed up as this is not out of place. Go straight to the unknowing Rabite and click the B tab to launch your technique on the Rabite. This way, you will achieve almost two times the destruction you inflict on an enemy.

We cannot continue until you understand the two things we are about to tell you. Each time there is an adjustment in the HP, the increase or decrease in the HP will be written over the game page in large numbers. Also, the HP has four colours and each of them have their peculiar significance.

Purple: This signifies the destruction inflicted on an opponent.

Red: This signifies the destruction inflicted on an associate.

Yellow: This signifies the healing received by an opponent.

Green: This signifies the healing received by an associate.

You should have also seen by now that the amount of experience you earn from a kill and the opponent's stage in game show up on the game page. They are helpful and you must strive to be equal in stage with the opponents in your area. Battling against them when they are higher than you is not an easy task.

If you remember, the opening part of this walkthrough tells you that the game will be easy as long as you keep to the walkthrough. The necessity of obeying this walkthrough can never be over emphasized. You must constantly try to maintain equal practical knowledge with opponents or be higher than them.

We have given you the primary deals about battling in Trials of Mana, we can go over to your teammate and tour the Cave of Waterfalls.

Trails of Mana/Part 4: Take the Golden Brick Road

As you appear in the Free City, Maia, you must bear in mind that you are heading to Forcena. You will meet King Richard there and he will teach you all you should learn relating to Mana Stones. You have to start moving now as your journey will stretch over three chapters.

Purchase fresh caps for all your game personas and do not forget to store enough Round Drops and Angel Grails.

However, the Angel Grails should not be excess since you have to keep back some funds for the purchasing of good dwarven machine in a short while. Take your west out out of the town and you will meet a mariner. The mariner will inform you of the Priest of Light's sickness during the erection of a pillar. It is not agood news so you have to depart Maia and the Golden Road is where you will find yourself.

There are lots of Pororns and Killer Bugs on the Golden road. The road is a link between Maia and Merchant City Byzel. You will see the usefulness of the Merchant City Byzel when you get to the second phase in the game. At this point, the town is not open to non-indigenes because the ninjas, the sorcerers and the beastmen are raiding towns. This is none of your concern.

This part is a small portion of a bigger part and we will reward you with a cookie when you develop it. A cavern that has its destination as the Cleft of the Earth lies three game pages from Byzel. The Cleft of the Earth is a long narrow hole, the size of a very large snake and it goes through the division of the land demarcating Byzen and Maia from Forcena and the Molebear Highlands. That is your destination and you have to use the bridge that goes over it.

You will see a Silver Statue at the opening of the cavern while the new page has the bridge and the Cleft. Certain Altenians, with their Machine Golems will welcome you when you get to the bridge.

Boss: Two Machine Golems

Although Machine Golems have their strength, the two before you are not so powerful. Where Angela is a member of your team, employ her Holy Ball on the Machine Golems as they have no defence spells. You can use Carlie's Heal Light (she must have perfected it at this point), or continue to prevent a low HP when Carlie is not in your team. Watch out for the Drill Punch offense that comes from the Machine Golems and avoid them as soon as they start to sparkle in red.

The toughest offense the Machine Golems can give is the Rocket Launcher. It kills game personas that already had low life as it inflicts destruction of 80 to 90 on its enemy.

They do not always employ this offense; they often set it off frequently while battling with you. You have to be at alert so you can click on your equipment list as soon as they set it off. You might be lucky to have selected Assassin Bug Eyes before so this is where they help you. The Bug Eyes are very powerful and continuous use kills the Machine Golems with destruction worth 90 HP.

The other Golem will eventually destroy itself as well as the bridge so you have to find another route to Forcena. All you can do is to return to Maia.

Trials of Mana/Part 5: A Gneed for Gnome

Take a break to relax and store your game. After that, walk over to the building on the far east of Maia. Speak with the Frenchman who is somewhat stout when you get into the building. The stout Frenchman's name is Bon Voyage and keeps a heavy-calibre gun at the back of his building. After speaking with him, you will go back with him outside but keep your mind ready for a letdown. There is no gunpowder in the gun so you have to find it.

At the entrance of the guesthouse, you will see a NPC who has red beard on his face and bald head. Speak to him first before going out to return to the Cleft of the Earth. The NPC will not inform you of the coming section so go over to speak to the Silver Statue and then make use of Wisp. The wall will come apart to create an opening and show you a different route.

Walk into the underground passage and ensure to remember the paths going over the staircases.

It is only a short time before you have to race through them. Take the road leading to the dwarf village when you get to the end of the passage.

You will find the dwarf village to be quite interesting. Find your way to the equipment store to see Watts, the storekeeper. The gunpowder is in Watt's possession but Watts is not in the store so you have to help yourself out. Move down to the arms store to get yourself fortified and restock necessary items with the remaining money you have. Take a break to relax and store you game before leaving.

You will see a dwarf making a hole in the ground as soon as you leave the dwarf village. Take the underground passage he digs for you after you have spoken with him. Continue down the passage and you will meet a dwarf, Watts. However, going to him is not possible so take the west and go through the road on the north. Continue down the road till you see Watts on his feet in a clear room. You can finally get close to him. Speak with him and he will tell you the price of the Gunpowder is 5,000 gil.

You cannot afford it yet but don't worry about it because Watts will take to his heels a second time. This time, you have to trail behind him and maintain the passage way till you get to get to the where it ends and you and Watts will be together in a room. Restore your health and speak with him to begin the battle with the boss.

> **Boss**: Jewel Eater

You will find this boss as extra powerful when he is higher than you. Given that you have been playing a good game, you should be in your sixth stage and you will be able to handle the battle. You are not equipped with Thunder Magic which the Jewel Eater has low resistance to, so maintain your usual offense strikes. Every of Angela's MP should be spent on Holy Ball and the Assassin Bug Eyes will also be helpful here. They can only work when you selected them earlier as a part of your team. Continue hitting the Jewel Eater and maintaining HP of nothing less than 70. The Jewel Eater has a sorcery menu that contains Defense Up and Diamond Missile. As he draws near to his death, he will start to use his Defense Up.

Gnome will come to you when you have defeated the Jewel Eater. He will come with a tale to narrate to you and later becomes a part of your group. Watt will express regret for his initial actions and then let you have the Gunpowder. Your mission here is over; destination Forcena is now feasible.

Five Hacks in Choosing from Difficult Options

Lovers of Square Enix are always impressed by it. Square Enix has released two upgrades on the '90s traditional RPGs although we are barely six months into the year. Trials of Mana is going to be a new adventure for the lovers of Square Enix in the West since its first release last year was specially for the Japanese lovers. You will be intrigued with how detailed the game is and you will be actively engaged in making tough decisions. This series has been improved with better battles, better computer and human interaction and more effective functions. We have compiled certain hacks that will help you have an interesting experience.

1. Zero Bad Decisions

The number one law in Trials of Mana is that your choice can never be wrong. Any option you select leads you to a whole exciting adventure. Whether you are contemplating between the light lesson and dark lesson or the game personas to include in your team, feel free to make your choice. You will surely have an awesome experience.

2. Game Persona Perspective

Yes, the game does not recognize any decision as a wrong one. Still, your decisions should be based on fully fledged considerations. One thing you must know is that to main characters have same deadly opponent. The plot of your game is dependent on the major enemy.

Crimson Wizard is the opponent of Angela and Duran and he in charge of the raiding of Valsena Kingdom by the Altena Nation.

Hawkeye and Riesz have Belladonna as their opponent and she leads the band of robbers to secretly enter Laurant in her position as their captain.

Charlotte and Kevin are to battle against the Soul Devourer who is known as Goremand. Goremand is an accomplice to the Ferolia beastmen who raid the Holy City Wendel as well as many other towns.

All the game personas are citizens of the towns in the game, some to towns that raid others and some to towns that are raided by others. Your choice of major game personas controls the plot line of your game play. Still, the only way for you to see everything fully is for you to include the second major character in your group.

Therefore, a group that has Duran with Angela and Charlotte will see the complete narrative of the raid carried out by Altena under the Crimson Wizard. Sadly, it will not have access to some stories about Goremand and there will be completely nothing relating to Belladonna.

The last prison and the villain of your play will also be a result of your major character choices.

There are useful tests on traits that you can take on the authorized Trials of Mana page to help you select characters. Another option is to cast a die with appropriate amount of sides to help pick a game persona.

3. Explore Competencies

While you play the game, you begin to gain sets of personal Chain Abilities and Character Abilities which will be helpful to all major characters. These abilities become yours when you boost stats or get them from NPCs you meet all around the game. The tiny step up they give has the ability to totally switch fight sides.

Ensure to be friendly when you see them till you see a loadout that interests you.

With Charlotte or Angela in your party, abilities that surpass magic can throw the enemy off balance. With warriors like Kevin or Duran, you should have counter ability and toughness.

The key is to allocate your money wisely to give your all game personas abilities capable of shooting up the CS meter.

Trials of Mana was well known because of its many professional tutorials. Major adjustments come when you swap lessons, coupled with the fun that comes with it. Every game persona is to undergo two lessons in stage two, four lessons in stage three and two after play lessons in stage four.

As you move to a new stage, you can decide to take the dark route or light route. In light lessons, the game personas are exposed to useful sorcery that includes how to restore health and enhance body while dark lessons teach how to throw attacks and break body enhancement magic. You can choose the lessons to suit how you love your games or you can decide to see a new method to game play.

Lastly, the next thing to do when you move to a new stage is to go to the Training menu and raise your stats. With this, there will be more lifts in trait you want to increase, you will have access to more competencies and you will gain more sorcery skills. Your focus should be on the major stats of your game personas alongside Spirit. It is the Spirit that makes you eligible for new sorcery skills. You can also store points before you swap lessons so you can know the sorcery skills and competencies you will meet there.

As the game goes on, you will be given the opportunity to change restore your original lessons and stats in case you get inclined to a new lesson.

4. Memorize your menus

Trials of Mana is similar to Secret of Mana where both of them have round menus. You can pause your game or choose a magic or equipment you need by clicking up or down on your D-pad.

You have to fortify your equipment to the round menu when you are away from a battle. Do not wait to begin a boss battle before you fortifying your Faerie Walnuts or Chocolates, if they are required. As soon as a fight begins, you are eligible to just nine pieces of each weapon. This way, gamers cannot purchase excess Cups of Wishes to enable them always win battles. When the fight is over, your numbers will adjust, but this can only happen when there is nothing less than nine in your stock.

You might appreciate a cheat to have less hectic fights: Getting an equipment or sorcery from the round menu slows down the action of the game persona involved for a few seconds. The trick is to involve main characters who are not in the fight when getting anything from the round menu. Using a battle of Riesz, Angela and Kevin against a villain as an instance, Kevin has to be your hero then take up the round menu and strike ZR or ZL to cross over to the round menu of your associate.

That way, you will be able to use Risez to enhance the group and use Angela to throw dangerous offense magic. Also, Kevin avoids the slowing down part and can throw blows repeatedly to destroy the villain. However, ensure your associates are protected from enemy hits to prevent any distraction for you.

5. Develop Seeds

Trials of Mana have a mysterious but interesting part which is the Item Seeds. They are in treasure boxes and round vessels no matter where you are located. They are released by opponents and most times, they become yours when you investigate sparking balls. You are to sow the seeds anytime you are in a guesthouse and you will be rewarded with different equipment.

The more seeds you sow, the more experience goes into your plant vase. With this, your plant vase upgrades and lets you get higher graded seeds and higher materials from them. Getting a high number of Li'l Cactus makes him generate the li'l raise on his own. This way, your chances of getting a worthy reward are higher.

There is no point in making extra effort to earn several indefinite items when they are already provided for by the game. Serums can develop from your Item Seeds and they give an eternal increase to the stats of a main character.

Also, the probability of getting the utmost secret weapon for every game persona increases as soon as your plant vase moves to stage four.

Any item can develop from any Item Seed, yet a seed with higher grade gives you higher chances of better items. As you play further you will encounter an Item Seed that has the surety of better items, but for now the lesser items that are dropping should not bother you.

Made in the USA
Coppell, TX
15 May 2021